Origami Farm Animals

Gareth Stevens
Publishing

Please visit our website, www.garethstevens.com. For a free color catalog of all our high-quality books, call toll free 1-800-542-2595 or fax 1-877-542-2596.

Library of Congress Cataloging-in-Publication Data

Miles, Lisa.
    Origami farm animals / Lisa Miles.
      pages   cm. — (Amazing origami)
    Includes index.
    ISBN 978-1-4339-9653-5 (pbk.)
    ISBN 978-1-4339-9654-2 (6-pack)
    ISBN 978-1-4339-9652-8 (library binding)
    1. Origami—Juvenile literature. 2. Domestic animals—Juvenile literature. 3. Livestock—Juvenile literature.   I. Title.
    TT872.5.M554 2013
    736'.982—dc23

                                                                2012050328

First Edition

Published in 2014 by
Gareth Stevens Publishing
111 East 14th Street, Suite 349
New York, NY 10003

Copyright © 2014 Arcturus Publishing

Models and photography: Belinda Webster and Michael Wiles
Text: Lisa Miles
Design: Emma Randall
Editors: Anna Brett, Becca Clunes, and Joe Harris

Animal photography: Shutterstock

Printed in the United States of America

CPSIA compliance information: Batch #CS13GS: For further information contact Gareth Stevens, New York, New York at 1-800-542-2595.

Contents

Basic Folds

Origami has been popular in Japan for hundreds of years and is now loved all around the world. You can make great origami models with just one sheet of paper... and this book shows you how!

The paper used in origami is thin but strong, so that it can be folded many times. It is usually colored on one side. You can also use ordinary scrap paper, but make sure it's not too thick.

Origami models often share the same folds and basic designs, known as "bases." This introduction explains some of the folds and bases that you will need for the projects in this book. When making the models, follow the key below to find out what the lines and arrows mean. And always crease well!

KEY

valley fold ------------	step fold (mountain and valley fold next to each other)	direction to move paper ⤷
mountain fold		push ◄

MOUNTAIN FOLD

To make a mountain fold, fold the paper so that the crease is pointing up toward you, like a mountain.

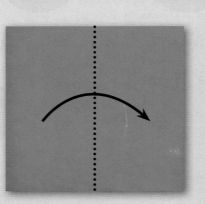

VALLEY FOLD

To make a valley fold, fold the paper the other way, so that the crease is pointing away from you, like a valley.

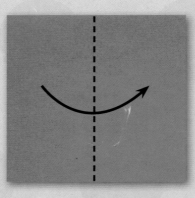
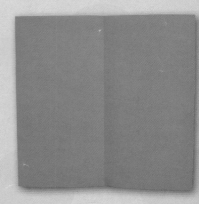

INSIDE REVERSE FOLD

An inside reverse fold is useful if you want to make a nose or a tail, or if you want to flatten the shape of another part of an origami model.

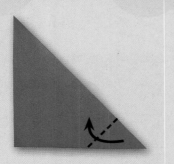

Open

1 Practice by first folding a piece of paper diagonally in half. Make a valley fold on one point and crease.

2 It's important to make sure that the paper is creased well. Run your finger over the crease two or three times.

3 Unfold and open up the corner slightly. Refold the crease nearest to you into a mountain fold.

4 Open up the paper a little more and then tuck the tip of the point inside. Close the paper. This is the view from the underside of the paper.

5 Flatten the paper. You now have an inside reverse fold.

OUTSIDE REVERSE FOLD

An outside reverse fold is useful if you want to make a head, beak, foot, or another part of your model that sticks out.

1 Practice by first folding a piece of paper diagonally in half. Make a valley fold on one point and crease.

2 It's important to make sure that the paper is creased well. Run your finger over the crease two or three times.

3 Unfold and open up the corner slightly. Refold the crease farthest away from you into a valley fold.

Open

4 Open up the paper a little more and start to turn the corner inside out. Then close the paper when the fold begins to turn.

5 You now have an outside reverse fold. You can either flatten the paper or leave it rounded out.

Bases

WATERBOMB BASE

① Start with a square of paper, the point turned toward you. Make two diagonal valley folds.

② The paper should now look like this. Turn it over.

③ Make two valley folds along the horizontal and vertical lines.

Push  Push

④ Push the paper into this shape, so the center spot pops up.

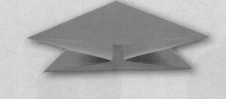

⑤ Push the sides in, bringing the back and front sections together.

⑥ Flatten the paper. You now have a waterbomb base.

KITE BASE

① Start with the point turned toward you. Valley fold it in half diagonally.

② Valley fold the left section to meet the center crease.

③ Do the same on the other side.

④ You now have a kite base.

FISH BASE

1 Make a kite base, as shown on page 6. Valley fold the left corner.

2 Do the same on the other side.

3 The paper should now look like this.

open

4 Open out the top left corner. Take hold of the inside flap and pull it down to meet the center crease to make a new flap, as shown.

open

5 Flatten the paper. Then do the same on the other side.

6 You now have a fish base.

Pig

This cute origami pig stands up on its four pointy feet.
A pig's feet are called hooves.

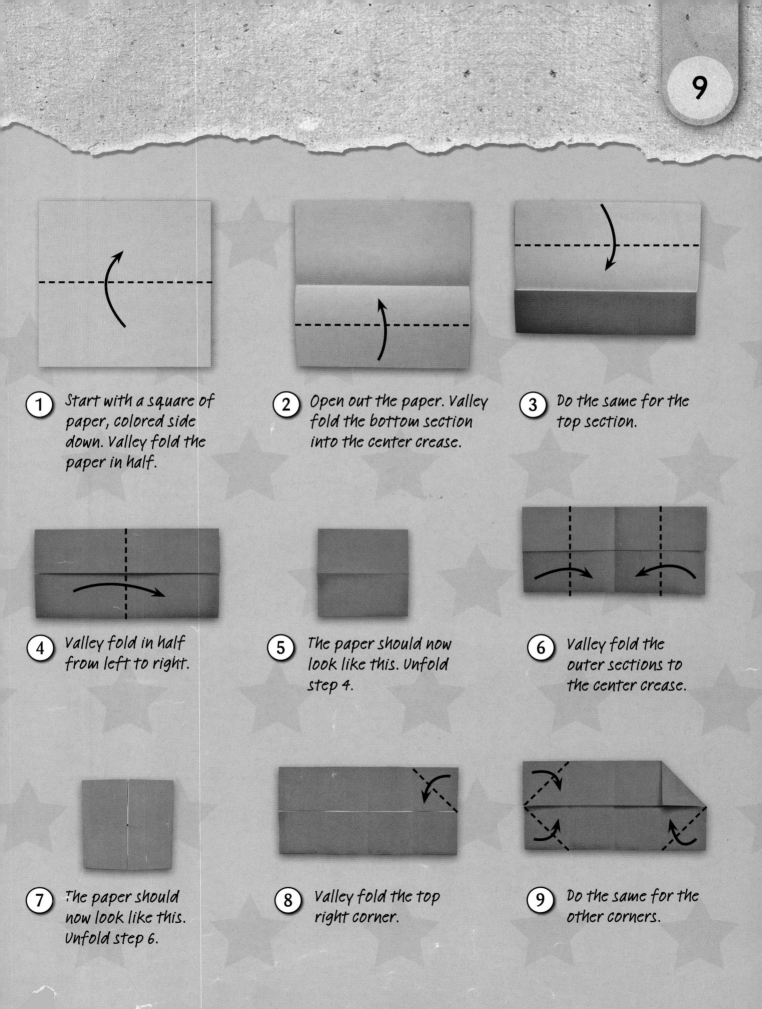

1 Start with a square of paper, colored side down. Valley fold the paper in half.

2 Open out the paper. Valley fold the bottom section into the center crease.

3 Do the same for the top section.

4 Valley fold in half from left to right.

5 The paper should now look like this. Unfold step 4.

6 Valley fold the outer sections to the center crease.

7 The paper should now look like this. Unfold step 6.

8 Valley fold the top right corner.

9 Do the same for the other corners.

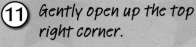

Open up

(10) The paper should now look like this.

(11) Gently open up the top right corner.

(12) Flatten it down into a triangle. Do the same for the other corners.

(13) Mountain fold the paper in half, so that the bottom folds under the top.

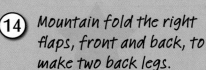

(14) Mountain fold the right flaps, front and back, to make two back legs.

(15) Repeat step 14 to make two front legs.

Did You Know?

Pigs are very intelligent animals. They can learn how to perform tricks faster than dogs!

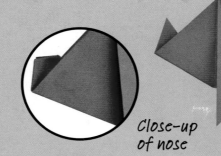

16 Mountain fold the right point.

17 Unfold, then make an inside reverse fold to create the tail. Now mountain fold the left point.

Close-up of tail

18 Unfold, then make an inside reverse fold to create the nose. Tuck the end inside to make it blunt.

Close-up of nose

19 Now stand your origami pig up on its hooves!

Duck

The duck spends most of its time swimming in lakes and ponds. Its feathers are so waterproof that when it dives underwater, the top layer of feathers keeps the others dry.

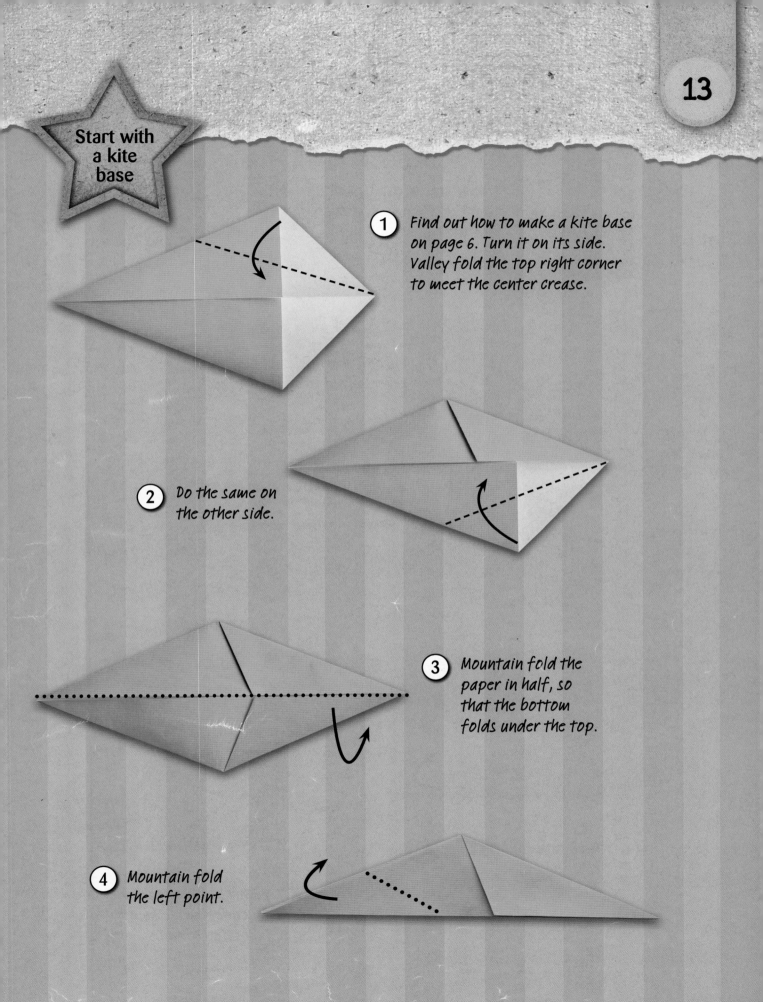

Start with a kite base

1. Find out how to make a kite base on page 6. Turn it on its side. Valley fold the top right corner to meet the center crease.

2. Do the same on the other side.

3. Mountain fold the paper in half, so that the bottom folds under the top.

4. Mountain fold the left point.

Did You Know?

When ducks build nests, they use their own feathers to make a warm, soft cushion for their eggs.

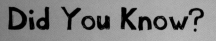

5 Unfold, then make an inside reverse fold to create the neck.

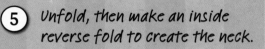

6 Mountain fold the right point.

7 Unfold, then make an inside reverse fold to create the tail.

8 Mountain fold the left point.

9 Unfold, then make an inside reverse fold to create the head.

10 Balance the model upright. Now you have a little origami duck, ready to swim away!

Rooster

A rooster is a male chicken. He has long, impressive tail feathers, which he uses to help him show off to the females. Check out this origami rooster's tail.

Start with a kite base

1. Find out how to make a kite base on page 6. Valley fold the right corner to the center crease.

2. Do the same on the other side.

3. Mountain fold the paper in half along the center crease, so that the left side goes behind the right.

Flaps are on the left.

4. Turn the paper on its side. Mountain fold the right point.

5. Unfold, then make an outside reverse fold to create the neck.

Did You Know?

Cock-a-doodle-do! Roosters are famous for crowing at daybreak. However, they also crow through the rest of the day.

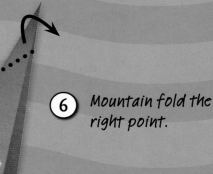

6 Mountain fold the right point.

7 Unfold, then make an inside reverse fold to create the tail.

8 Mountain fold the right point.

9 Unfold, then make an outside reverse fold to create the tail feather.

10 Mountain fold the left point.

11 Unfold, then make an inside reverse fold to create the head.

12 Mountain fold the head.

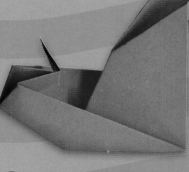

13 Unfold and make another inside reverse fold to create the beak.

14 Now you have an origami rooster with a splendid tail!

Rabbit

Medium

The rabbit has sensitive ears that can be turned in any direction to pick up sounds. Here's how to make an origami version—complete with long ears!

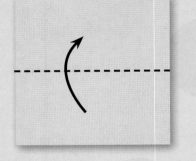

1. Take a piece of paper and valley fold as shown, then open it out again.

2. Valley fold the bottom section up to meet the center crease.

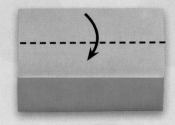

3. Do the same for the top section.

4. Valley fold the right corner.

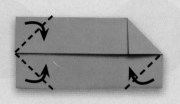

5. Valley fold the other corners in the same way.

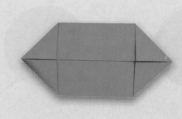

6. The paper should now look like this.

7. Open out the corner folds.

Open up

8. Gently pull out the right corner. Tuck the center fold inside to create a flap.

9. The paper should now look like this.

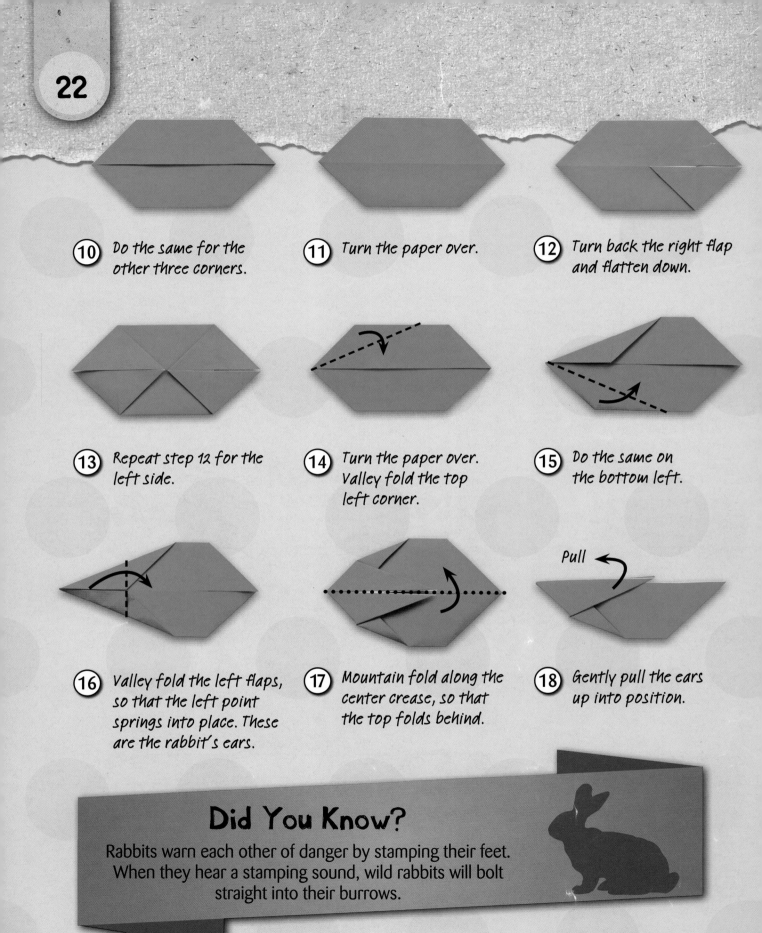

10 Do the same for the other three corners.

11 Turn the paper over.

12 Turn back the right flap and flatten down.

13 Repeat step 12 for the left side.

14 Turn the paper over. Valley fold the top left corner.

15 Do the same on the bottom left.

16 Valley fold the left flaps, so that the left point springs into place. These are the rabbit's ears.

17 Mountain fold along the center crease, so that the top folds behind.

Pull

18 Gently pull the ears up into position.

Did You Know?

Rabbits warn each other of danger by stamping their feet. When they hear a stamping sound, wild rabbits will bolt straight into their burrows.

19 Flatten the paper. Mountain fold the right point.

20 Unfold, then make an inside reverse fold to create the feet. Mountain fold across the nose.

21 Unfold, then tuck in the nose.

22 Gently puff out the long ears to give them their shape—and you have your origami rabbit!

Horse

The horse is known for its speed and is one of the fastest mammals on land. It has four different types of movement—walking, trotting, cantering, and galloping!

Start with a fish base

① Find out how to make a fish base on page 7. Turn it so that the two flaps point to the right. Mountain fold the paper in half, so that the bottom section folds under the top.

② Mountain fold the left point upward.

③ Unfold, then make an inside reverse fold to create the neck.

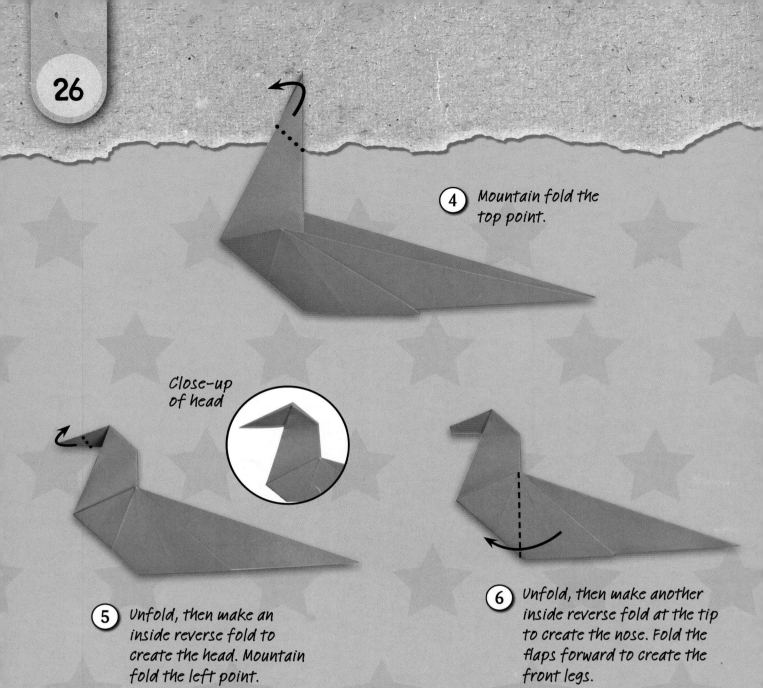

4 Mountain fold the top point.

Close-up of head

5 Unfold, then make an inside reverse fold to create the head. Mountain fold the left point.

6 Unfold, then make another inside reverse fold at the tip to create the nose. Fold the flaps forward to create the front legs.

Did You Know?

Horses come in very different sizes. Miniature horses are about 3 feet (0.9 m) tall. Shire horses are about 5.6 feet (1.7 m) tall.

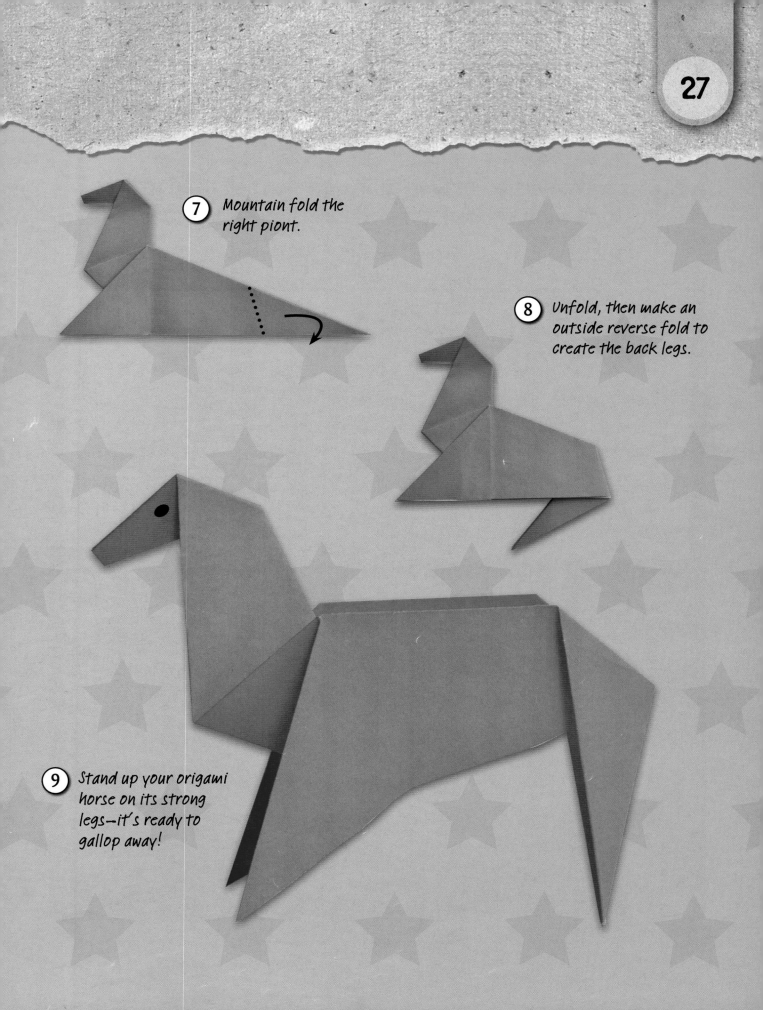

7 Mountain fold the right piont.

8 Unfold, then make an outside reverse fold to create the back legs.

9 Stand up your origami horse on its strong legs—it's ready to gallop away!

Cow

A cow spends most of its time eating grass. They need to eat and drink a huge amount to produce almost 9 gallons (34 l) of milk a day!

MAKE THE HEAD

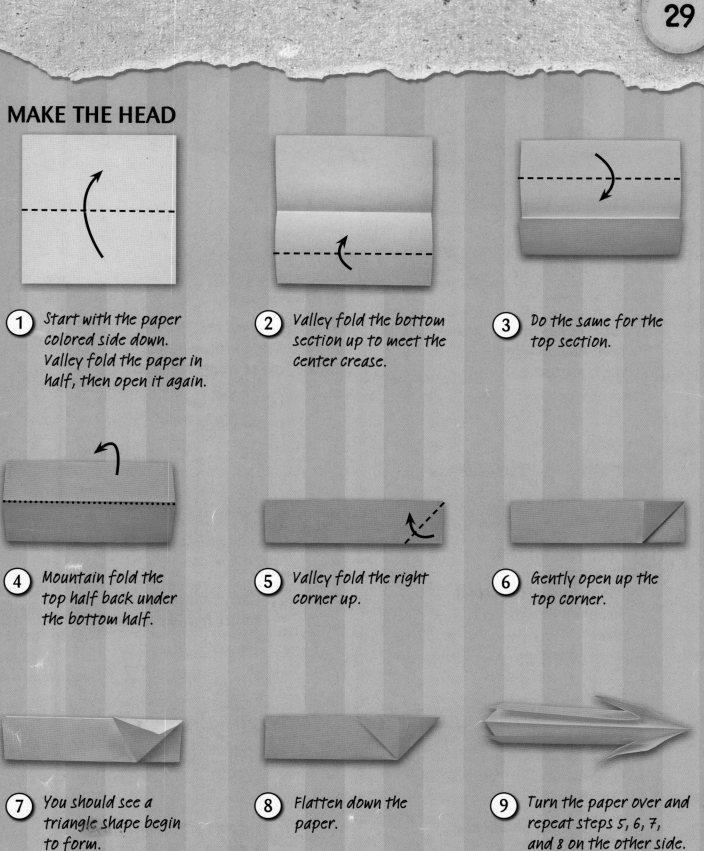

1 Start with the paper colored side down. Valley fold the paper in half, then open it again.

2 Valley fold the bottom section up to meet the center crease.

3 Do the same for the top section.

4 Mountain fold the top half back under the bottom half.

5 Valley fold the right corner up.

6 Gently open up the top corner.

7 You should see a triangle shape begin to form.

8 Flatten down the paper.

9 Turn the paper over and repeat steps 5, 6, 7, and 8 on the other side. From above, the paper looks like this.

Did You Know?

Cows only sleep for about 4 hours a day. However, they are able to snooze while standing up.

Close-up of nose

10 Turn the paper back over. Mountain fold the right tip.

11 Unfold, then tuck the tip back into the crease with an inside reverse fold to create the nose.

12 Valley fold the right corner of the flap to create ears on both sides. Mountain fold the left side.

13 Valley fold the bottom corner to make a triangle.

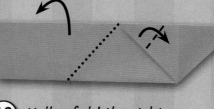

14 The paper should now look like this.

15 Unfold the triangle, then make an inside reverse fold for slotting onto the body.

MAKE THE BODY

⭐ Start with a waterbomb base

1 Find out how to make a waterbomb base on page 6. Valley fold the left tip.

2 Gently open the base from the right.

Open here

3 Continue opening the base. A triangle shape will appear at the top and bottom. Flatten them both down, as shown above.

4 Valley fold the paper in half from top to bottom.

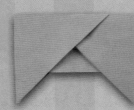

5 Turn the paper over. Mountain fold the left corner. Unfold, then make an inside reverse fold to shape the cow's body.

PUT THE COW TOGETHER

1 Slot the head into the body so that it grips firmly.

2 Your origami cow has its head bent down to graze on the tasty grass!

Glossary

base A simple, folded shape that is used as the starting point for many different origami projects.

burrow The underground home of a small animal, such as a rabbit.

crease A line in a piece of paper made by folding.

crow To make a loud cry.

graze To eat grass.

hoof The foot of a pig.

mammal A warm-blooded animal that gives birth to live young.

mountain fold An origami step where a piece of paper is folded so that the crease is pointing upward, like a mountain.

snooze To sleep lightly.

step fold A mountain fold and valley fold next to each other.

upright Standing up.

valley fold An origami step where a piece of paper is folded so that the crease is pointing downward, like a valley.

waterbomb A traditional origami shape, which can be filled with water.

Further Reading

Robinson, Nick. *Absolute Beginner's Origami*. New York: Potter Craft, 2006.

Robinson, Nick. *World's Best Origami*. New York: Alpha Books, 2010.

Van Sicklen, Margaret. *Origami on the Go: 40 Paper-Folding Projects for Kids Who Love to Travel*. New York: Workman Publishing Company, 2009.

Index